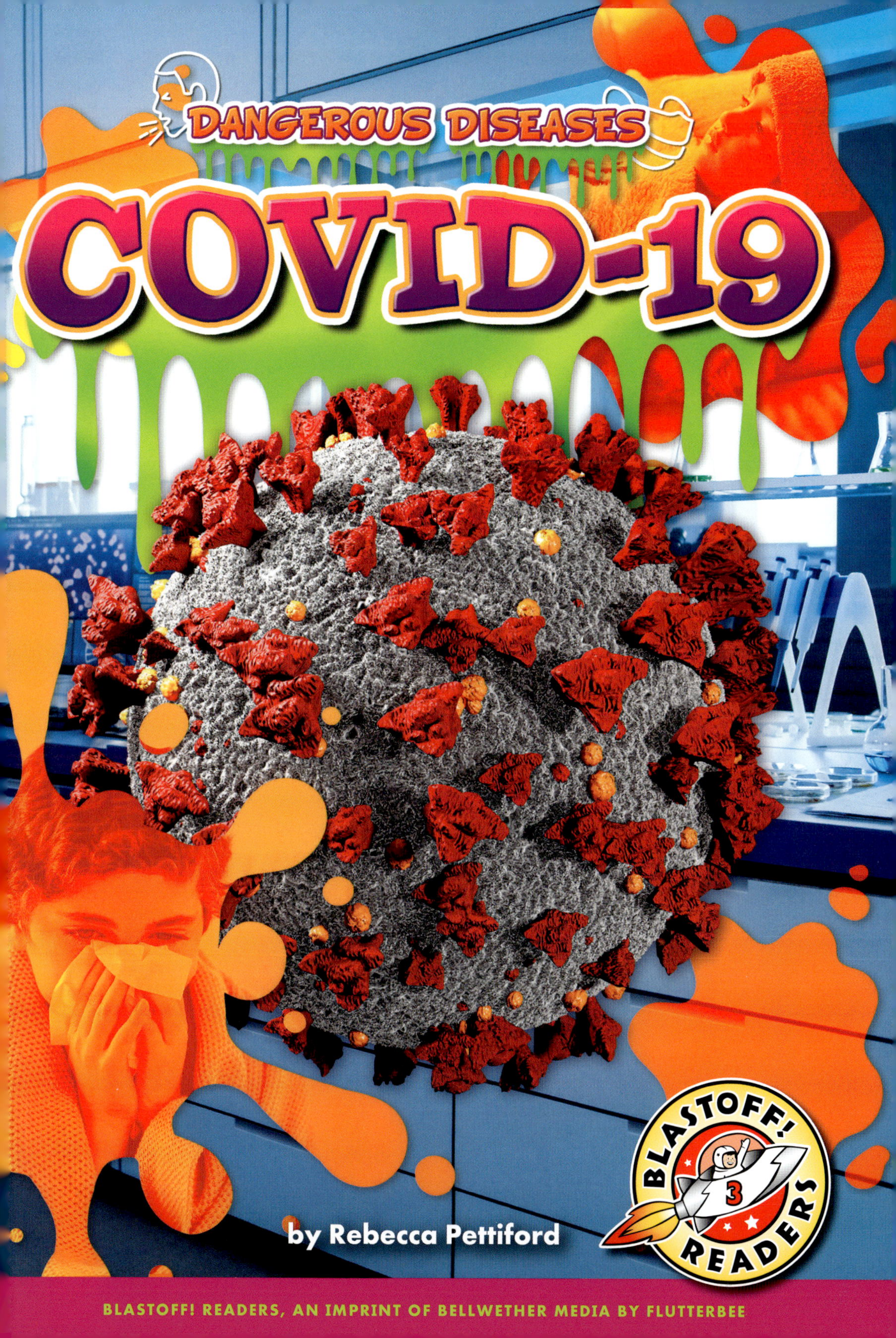
DANGEROUS DISEASES
COVID-19
by Rebecca Pettiford
BLASTOFF! READERS 3
BLASTOFF! READERS, AN IMPRINT OF BELLWETHER MEDIA BY FLUTTERBEE

Blastoff! Readers are carefully developed by literacy experts to build reading stamina and move students toward fluency by combining standards-based content with developmentally appropriate text.

Level 1 provides the most support through repetition of high-frequency words, light text, predictable sentence patterns, and strong visual support.

Level 2 offers early readers a bit more challenge through varied sentences, increased text load, and text-supportive special features.

Level 3 advances early-fluent readers toward fluency through increased text load, less reliance on photos, advancing concepts, longer sentences, and more complex special features.

★ **Blastoff! Universe**

Reading Level

Blastoff! Beginners — Grade K → Blastoff! Readers — Grades 1–3 → Blastoff! Discovery — Grade 4

This edition first published in 2027 by Bellwether Media, Inc.

For information regarding permission, write to Bellwether Media, Inc., Attention: Permissions Department, 3500 American Blvd W, Suite 150, Bloomington, MN 55431.

Library of Congress Cataloging-in-Publication Data is available at www.loc.gov or upon request from the publisher.

ISBN: 9798898800642 (hardcover)
ISBN: 9798898801885 (ebook)

Editor: Suzane Nguyen Designer: Brittany McIntosh

Printed in the United States of America, North Mankato, MN.

Table of Contents

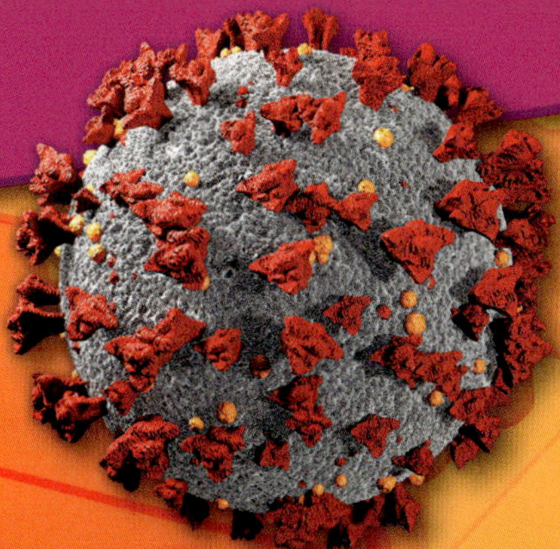

What Is COVID-19?

COVID-19 is a very **contagious** illness. People of all ages can get it.

It is named after a **coronavirus** that first appeared in 2019. A serious form of this **virus** causes COVID-19.

Anyone can get COVID-19. Signs include **fever**, coughing, shortness of breath, and a runny nose. Some people cannot taste or smell.

Long-term Effects

Some people can still feel sick for months after getting COVID-19. This is called long COVID. Signs include headaches and tiredness.

headaches

tiredness

Since 2019, over seven million people around the world have died from COVID-19.

History of COVID-19

Wuhan, China

COVID-19 began in Wuhan, China, in late 2019. It likely started in animals. In January 2020, the first cases of COVID-19 appeared outside China.

In March 2020, COVID-19 became a **pandemic**.

People helped one another
during the pandemic.
They wore masks. They practiced
social distancing.

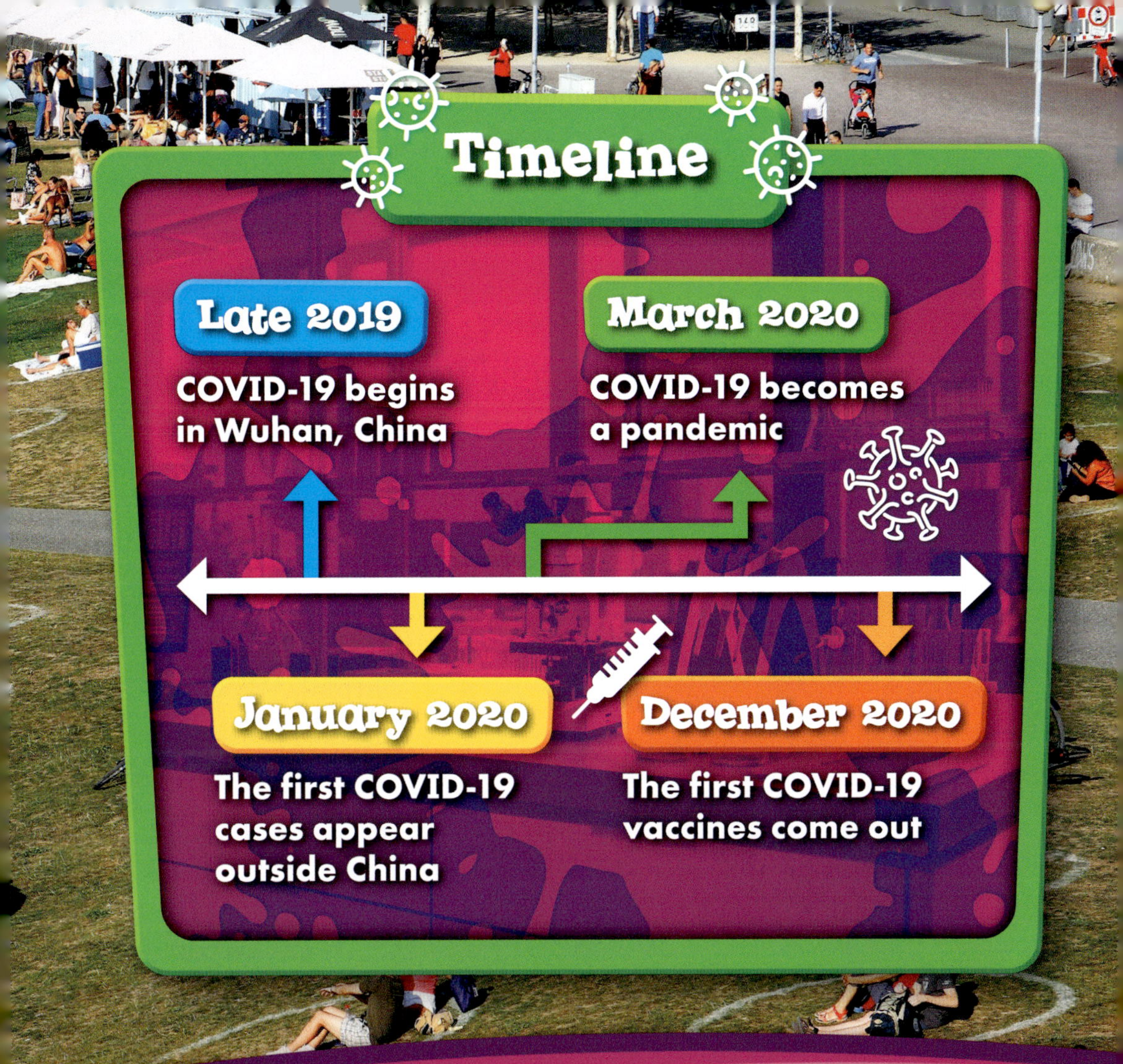

Health care workers took care of the sick. Many places went into **lockdown**. The first **vaccines** came out in December 2020.

How Does COVID-19 Spread?

COVID-19 spreads when a person with COVID-19 coughs or sneezes. Droplets from the cough or sneeze can spread to someone nearby.

People get sick when droplets enter the mouth, nose, or eyes.

Sick people may touch things like door handles, tables, and other objects. They leave the virus behind.

Healthy people can get sick after they touch the objects.

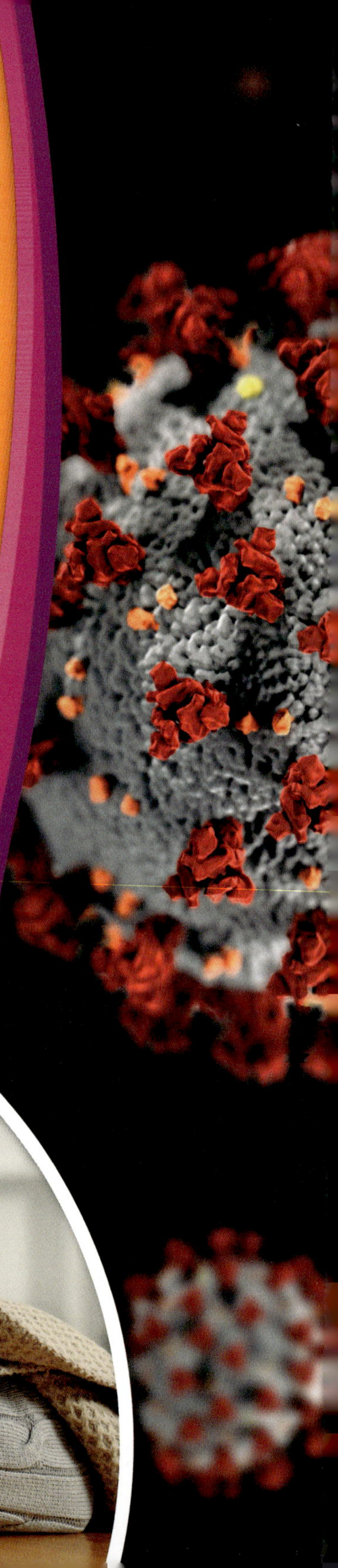

How COVID-19 Spreads

By Air

1 

Someone coughs or sneezes.

2 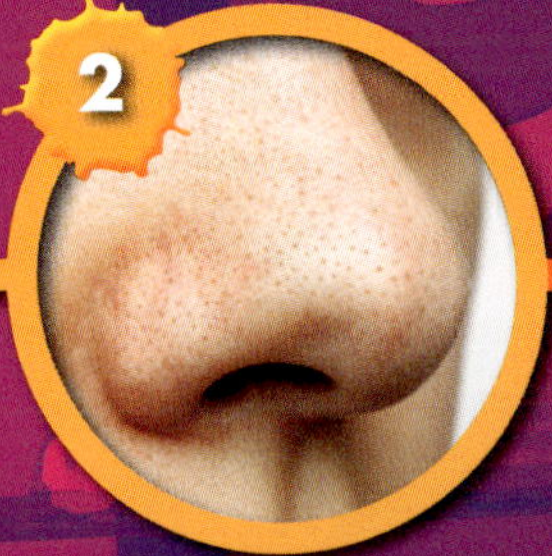

Droplets in the air enter a person's mouth or nose.

3 

Person gets COVID-19.

By Touch

1 

Virus on object.

2 

Person touches object.

3 

Person gets COVID-19.

Prevention and Treatment

A vaccine is the best way to stay safe. It helps the **immune system** make **antibodies**. They fight the illness!

People should also wash their hands and wear masks to stay safe.

Healing Heroes

Names

Doctor Katalin Karikó and Doctor Drew Weissman

Year Helped

2020

How They Helped

Worked together to help make the COVID-19 vaccine

If people get COVID-19, it can take 14 days for signs to appear.

Most people get better with rest. Taking **medicine** can help too. It can take several weeks to get better.

Millions of people have been impacted by COVID-19. It gave some people new health problems. Other people lost their businesses during the lockdown.

There is no cure for COVID-19 yet. People do their best to stay well!

avril
ZADIG TEAM
WORLDWIDE

Glossary

antibodies–materials that the body makes to fight illnesses

contagious–able to spread

coronavirus–a family of viruses that causes different illnesses; COVID-19 is caused by the coronavirus.

fever–a higher-than-normal body temperature

immune system–the system that protects the body from illnesses

lockdown–a short-term measure in which people cannot enter or leave an area or building

medicine–something taken to treat an illness

pandemic–the wide spread of an illness

social distancing–keeping a safe distance from other people

vaccines–a substance that is put into the body to help fight off an illness; a person who has gotten the vaccine is vaccinated.

virus–a tiny living thing that causes illness in people, animals, and plants

To Learn More

AT THE LIBRARY

Becker, Trudy. *COVID-19.* Mendota Heights, Minn.: Apex Editions, 2024.

Kukla, Lauren. *I'm a Doctor.* Rochester, Minn.: Mayo Clinic Press Kids, 2024.

Troupe, Thomas Kingsley. *What Would Happen If You Never Got Vaccines?* Mankato, Minn.: Amicus Learning, 2024.

ON THE WEB

FACTSURFER

Factsurfer.com gives you a safe, fun way to find more information.

1. Go to www.factsurfer.com.
2. Enter "COVID-19" into the search box and click 🔍.
3. Select your book cover to see a list of related content.

Index

The images in this book are reproduced through the courtesy of: Yury, front cover (hero), p. 3; PeopleImages, front cover (splatter left, splatter right), p. 7 (right); Gorodenkoff, front cover (back); Ahmet Misirligul, p. 4; Harbucks, p. 5; Billion Photos, p. 5 (inset); Chanintorn.v, p. 6; pics five, p. 7 (left); Hao Wan, p. 8; estherpoon, p. 9; Tupungato, pp. 10-11; Prostock-studio, p. 12; narvikk, p. 12 (inset); Photoroyalty, p. 13; New Africa, p. 14; Mauro Rodrigues, pp. 14-15; Pixel-Shot, p. 15 (by air 1); Marina Demeshko, p. 15 (by air 2); Pongchart B, p. 15 (by air 3); brizmaker, p. 15 (by touch 1); Zhuravlev Andrey, p. 15 (by touch 2); Xavier Lorenzo, p. 15 (by touch 3); Ground Picture, p. 16; ustas7777777, p. 16 (inset); Stephen J. Boitano/ Contributor/ Getty Images, p. 17; Art_Photo, p. 18; Yuliia Kaveshnikova, p. 19; fizkes, p. 20; Keitma, pp. 20-21.